THE TEN COMMANDMENTS

A COMMON MAN'S OPINION

P. L. Reynolds

Contents

INTRODUCTION TO
THE TEN COMMANDMENTS,
A COMMON MANS OPINION

This opinion was written as a straight up analysis of one of the most important documents ever given to, and recorded by, Man. The Ten Commandments is not only key to all of western civilization, but is also key to each individual life. It is about the relationship of God to Mankind and the relationship of man to man. It is about the relationship of God to each of us.

I did not preconceive or plan to write about such an important reality, an event, a communication between God and Man, I am just compelled to do so - for better or worse.

This opinion is written in the simplest manner possible in respect to the simple and direct way that the Commandments were given to us.

There have been other opinions written in the past, and today, by scholars and intellectuals and clergy.* This opinion is written by a layman who likes to think and contemplate realities that have come into our lives.

I think that, in the Commandments, God is speaking directly to us, the individual. Each of us. I feel God wants our direct communication and our direct love. No one is our representative. This is between God and each of us.

And so, God gave us the Ten Commandments to contemplate and act on. Men have named - these words of God - Commandments. While working on this Opinion, I began to feel that these are not commandments as we would normally think that a commandment is, but wishes that God has for us. Each statement is a wish, a want, that God has for each of us. God could stomp it into our head ...but He doesn't. There is a reason for that. The fact that He could but doesn't is really part of the understanding that we must come to.

I know this, the message is simple and straight forward so that all people, each of us, can achieve an understanding, a relationship, a revelation in and with God, our Creator. He talks to us in a way that He knows we can understand. He asks us to live and act in ways that He knows we can do.

I find in the words - of the Commandments - that God gave us, a certain revelation of HIM. A reflection of His reality. Each word can be contemplated - to find its own truth. Each word-relation to each other, can be contemplated to find a certain revelation. All of the words written, are about understanding, and relationship and revelation, that are dependent on the words and beyond the words. I feel that there are revelations about God and revelations about what God hopes for us in the Commandments.

The Commandments, it seems to me, are a crack in the hard wired evolutionary* circular paths that makes changes constantly, but still remains the same, as it progresses through time.

The Commandments are the first step in the ascendancy of Man to more than just animal. Love beyond the meager understanding of Man is confronting us in the Commandments. It is telling us that we can understand.

God is challenging us to answer the call. If only we will

hear. And act.

THE TEN COMMANDMENTS

THE TEN COMMANDMENTS

"I THE LORD AM YOUR GOD WHO
BROUGHT YOU OUT OF THE LAND OF
EGYPT, THE HOUSE OF BONDAGE: YOU
SHALL HAVE NO OTHER GODS BESIDE
ME."
Exodus 20:1

"YOU SHALL NOT MAKE FOR YOURSELF
A SCULPTURED IMAGE, OR ANY
IMAGE, OR ANY OF WHAT IS IN THE
HEAVENS ABOVE, OR THE EARTH
BELOW, OR ON THE WATERS UNDER
THE EARTH."
Exodus20:4

"YOU SHALL NOT SWEAR FALSELY BY
THE NAME OF THE LORD THY GOD;
FOR THE LORD WILL NOT CLEAR ONE
WHO SWEARS FALSELY BY HIS NAME."
Exodus 20:7

"REMEMBER THE SABBATH DAY AND
KEEP IT HOLY."
Exodus 20:8

"HONOR YOUR FATHER AND YOUR MOTHER, THAT YOU MAY LONG ENDURE ON THE LAND THAT THE LORD YOUR GOD IS GIVING YOU."
Exodus 20:12

"YOU SHALL NOT MURDER."
Exodus 20:13

"YOU SHALL NOT COMMIT ADULTERY."
Exodus 20:13

"YOU SHALL NOT STEAL."
Exodus 20:13

"THOU SHALL NOT BEAR FALSE WITNESS."
Exodus 20:14

"YOU SHALL NOT COVET YOUR NEIGHBOR'S HOUSE: YOU SHALL NOT COVET YOUR NEIGHBOR'S WIFE, OR HIS MALE OR FEMALE SLAVE, OR HIS OX OR HIS ASS, OR ANYTHING THAT IS YOUR NEIGHBOR'S."
Exodus 20:14

The First Commandment

"I THE LORD AM YOUR GOD WHO BROUGHT YOU OUT OF THE LAND OF EGYPT, THE HOUSE OF BONDAGE: YOU SHALL HAVE NO OTHER GODS BESIDE ME."
Exodus 20:1

God said, "I", to us. When He addressed us, He chose us, His People. And so He is. And so He did.

I respond to this First Commandment as, there is just God, as proclaimed by God. In other words, God has specifically said that He is the only One. There are no other gods. There is only Him. There is only God that our holy relationship is with. God Himself has proclaimed this Himself, to us, His people. Remember, we were His people when we were just lowly slaves, coming out of the land of Egypt. We have been chosen by the One who has created all things, including us.

We have to remember that we were chosen, and are continuously, chosen by God. There is a clue given when Moses asked God what His name is.* God said, tell them my name is, "I Am". The meaning in the ancient text translated, "I am becoming". The clue then, is that God is not stagnant or fixed but that He is ever becoming, ever more, ever expanding, ever all expansive.... . Really, there are no words to enclose God and God gave us that clue to contemplate and become, also, a part of that, that is Him. "I can't be enclosed or defined by, and put in a box by, a name", He said, in so many words. And so, as God Himself is ever becoming, He has told us that He has chosen us, and that there are no other gods, just Him. Think about it, He has chosen us, for all time, to be with Him. His choosing us makes us part of what He is. His choosing us tells us something about who we are and who we can be. His choosing us is telling us, that we are to be with Him for all time, as He is forever. So we naturally desire to be of God, if we want to be part of eternity. He has chosen us. He wants us to choose Him.

God Himself tells us that he is a jealous God. He does not want to lose us. What does He mean? I feel He means that, if we put anything, any thing, as more important in our hearts and minds and our every day attention, that it is not pleasing to Him. Some things go even further, I think, because some things become a sin or a sin in the making. I feel that, if we let anything become more important than the values that God Is, then we have put another god before Him. If, for example, we put our possessions as more important than our relationship with God, then we are down the wrong path and can be displeasing to God. That is what He has warned us against from the very beginning.

He tells us that He is a Jealous God. Jesus referred to this when he stated that we cannot have two masters. To put it simply, in our time, we can't put our possessions, our power, our entertainment, or any thing, in front of God. We cannot worship all of these things and worship God.

I think that, when we read or hear about idols from ancient times that we have a hard time relating to that. We know that they had little token idols and had large sculptures that they said represented their gods. In some ways it is difficult to transfer that to the time and the world that we live in. We don't have idols that we make and worship as the ancients did. As I think about it, though, there is very much idol worship in our present time all over the world, no country excluded. In some countries, that are extremely secular, and very materialistic, the possessions and power are the focus of daily life. More and more we don't give time to God. We say that we don't have time. In many places of worship, in the West, there are all kinds of idols, icons, that we use to remind us of God. None of this is what He wants. He has told us that very directly.*

And so, we are in the house of bondage. God will once again, have to lead us out of the house of bondage, to once again, purify and free us, on our path to revelation.

God, in choosing us, has asked us to join Him in His journey in Becoming. His choosing us, asks us, to have Faith in Him and to trust in Him. Could we say no? To God? I guess that we have, in so many ways, but God does not give up. He came to us before we knew what was going on. He is continually not giving up.

When God chose us, He chose to lead us out of the house of bondage. In doing this He has chosen to lead us to freedom. I feel that, all we have to do is follow. We may think that we want to have our possessions, but in the wrong state of being, we are possessed by our possessions. They become the "house of bondage" for us if achieved by the wrong means and valued in the wrong way. If we are leveraging out of our means to pay, if anything goes wrong, then this becomes our house of bondage. God has, and will, lead us from this house of bondage. We only have to be quiet and listen to Him.

God has given us life. He has given us unique life. He has made us all free in His sight. He has given us the freedom to choose Him or not. That being so, He has given each of us freedom in all things. If He can give it, then that is our state of being. He is asking us to receive Him. He has reached out to us first.

We did not even know that He existed until, out of the abyss, He told us that, "I am the Lord your God".

He is always, hoping, and waiting, on our response.

The Second Commandment

> **"YOU SHALL NOT MAKE FOR YOURSELF A SCULPTURED IMAGE, OR ANY IMAGE, OR ANY OF WHAT IS IN THE HEAVENS ABOVE, OR THE EARTH BELOW, OR ON THE WATERS UNDER THE EARTH."**
> Exodus20:4

This seems simple enough. Is it? First of all this is the second commandment. That in itself is very significant. Second only to God telling us that He is our God. Second only to God telling us that we have been chosen by Him. ("I am the Lord your God.") Why is this so important that it is second only to God telling us that He is our God? I feel that it is about God's expectation that we are to choose Him - that we are not to put anything in front of Him or before Him. So, I think that, it is our response to God's choosing us. We must also choose Him. We must choose Him for things to work out. Another way of saying this is, that we will simply be on our own until we do choose Him. God has chosen us but He has given us the free will to choose for ourselves. He knows, I believe, that is the way that we can be fulfilled in our discovery journey. He wants us to be the best that we can be. He tells us that we are worthy of Him - we just need to have Faith. Our lack of faith, and trust, leads us to replacing God with substitute things to rely on. Like a graven image.

What is graven and what is an image? Technically, a graven image is an image sculpted or made out of some material. Back then, most likely stone. It is also man made. I think that this can be extended to mean anything made by man, if we give it too much importance. If we worship it. "Man-made", is the key.

I believe that we are not to make any image that we use as a substitute in our worship. We are not to go through any image or person to communicate with God. God is telling us that He wants a direct relationship with us!

I also think that this second commandment is addressing a broader subject than just a simple graven image. It is really talking about putting anything or anyone before God. God is both telling us how much He loves us, His chosen, and telling us how we can be free, truly free. A graven image is the symbol of the false god and what we should not be worshipping.

So what can idols be? Anything that we place in front of God. Today, we don't make little stone idols like they did in ancient times but we have our own set of idols, images and people that we put our trust and love in. We are instructed by God to not put our trust in things or people or ideas in front of Him. God is our leader and our Father. He is telling us to not be limited by idols, or things, or people. He is a jealous God. He is jealous for our well being. He wants us to be the best we can be and He is revealing to us the path to follow.

He could have easily asked us to make an idol to Him, but He did not. I believe that there is a lot of significance in that.

Think about what that could possibly mean. He doesn't want to put us under His foot, or just make us be something that we don't understand in our revelation discovery. He doesn't want to control us so that we do what He wants whether we like it or not. Even though pleasing God would be good enough for us, He wants more than just that for us. Politicians and kings want to control us, but God does not, even though He could. Another thing - He does not want us to worship Him at a time and place and then go on down the road with the rest of our lives. He wants us to know that there is no time that He is not with us. He is always with us, at all places and time, as we are Becoming together. God and us. His people.

God is addressing us here because He is our God. He has chosen us as His people. He wants to free us from the falsehood of idol worship. We have had idols, from this ancient time, for 10,000 plus years. Longer than known countries have been around. So what's the problem? "We love our God and we just use these idols to remind us. Who knows, they might just bring us a little luck along the way." God, however, is a jealous God. He disagrees with getting a little luck. He tells us so. But why?

I believe that God does not want us to be distracted from the spiritual reality that He is. He can control all things but He gives us free will and He is concerned with us. He obviously wants us to go down the right path to spiritual revelation and enlightenment. Remember, God would not give His name to Moses because a name is a box that God cannot be contained in or defined by, or limited by. (It was particularly true in the ancient days when names had meaning.) If that is the case, He sure can't be contained in an image. But really, that is not the emphasis. He has chosen us and we are the emphasis. We are the ones that He is pushing on the discovery mission. I believe that, He is wanting us to concentrate on the reality that He is. He is wanting us to concentrate on the reality of what we can become. I am afraid that we are slow learners because we continue to fall backwards from the revelation that we are given. God, however, doesn't give up.

God had to overcome Man's reliance on superstition and idols in ancient times, during the time of idols and "gods". Man worshipped idols for thousands of years. God revealed His wishes to Moses during the Bronze age. During the Bronze age, at about 1450 BC, peoples were engrossed in nature spirits, superstition and various idols representing these spirits. These nature spirits were by far more important to people than each individual. Throughout ancient times human sacrifice was made to the "gods" to prove this point. People were subjugated by the spirits and by their leaders. Leaders were the powerful and the people, the individuals, were just not that important. God is, and has a different idea.

He is always telling us that we are important. That we are more important individually than any idol or leader. So what are idols today?

If you look at any pagan religion today you will find idol worship. I don't know of any pagan religion that does not have idol worship. For some reason, that I don't know, pagan religions seem to hold people back from developing. In some areas where primitive tribes live today, each tribe has its own idols. Each tribe eventually becomes the enemy of the neighboring tribes, who have their own idols. There are documentaries that display how barbarian they are to each other. A tribe member will kill a neighboring tribe member as though he is just an animal. Without remorse. There is no empathy or relationship to those outside of the tribe.

We know that God doesn't want this. He is trying to lead us to enlightenment. He has been trying for thousands of years. But we have our own ideas or idols that can lead to consequences. We have leaders who want to substitute our freedom in God to following whatever they decide is best for us. If we give in to this idol, and give away our responsibility, we are putting God in second place. We have our idols of possessions, self importance, position, being first or best, spiritual leaders that we follow first, technological wonders, dependence on materialism etc. I believe that God wants more than this for us.

So a simple little statement from God can lead to such wonderful revelations about Him and about ourselves. The revelation that I am most happy about is that God, the creator of all things, is interested in us. He wants us to be our best.

One other thought - God is also keeping us from making an idol out of Him. This is so significant. I believe that He must want us to be as He is. "I Am that I Am." "I shall be that I shall Be." With Him. His will be done.

The Third Commandment

> **"YOU SHALL NOT SWEAR FALSELY BY THE NAME OF THE LORD THY GOD; FOR THE LORD WILL NOT CLEAR ONE WHO SWEARS FALSELY BY HIS NAME."**
> Exodus 20:7

I believe that one of the profound ideas in this statement is the expectation that we are to treat God's name with reverence. We are at all times, to treat Him with reverence. In fact, this is the key to this commandment.

I believe that we should revere God as the center of our living. This doesn't mean that we all have to be priest or nuns but that our lives, whatever we do, is lived and done with God permeating our being. Which He is. It's as though God is sitting beside us and participating as we go, but also, more than that, God dwells in our very being, in every cell, in every atom, in the electromagnetism that keeps us together. Even unto infinity.

All of the Commandments have to be contemplated together. In the First Commandment we find that God has chosen us. In the Second Commandment we find that we are in a reciprocal relationship and that God expects certain response from us that indicates that we have chosen Him. He knows, but we are the ones struggling with revelation. There is every indication in the Commandments that God wants us to *know.* He wants us to *know!* He would have us *know.* The Creator of all things wants us to *know,* to be a part of the true knowledge, that He has created. He wants us to know the spiritual truths and reality of Being. He is after us to be complete. Completely attuned to all, as He is. Then we would be more attuned and at One with Him. Being attuned to completeness also means that there is a practical reality because we are physical beings, with a soul, as well as spiritual beings.

Our immediate practical reality would include the prohibitions that we usually associate with this commandment statement. Don't make or swear a false statement in the name of God or in reference to God. This is back to the idea of reverence for God, and his name. The opposite of revering God is the irreverent act of treating Him without reverence. That is, acting as though He is not here. Acting without His rules and advice. Using Gods name in vain. Swearing by His name. All of these things are the same as denying God. The fact that He asks us to "...not take the name in vain..." really implies more about what is not said than what is actually said. In a sense, all that exists is the name of God. The name is the defining thing. The name has a connection with physical reality, as it is an assurance of His being with us, as we are in this physical life. By revering His name we are also revering all that He creates. We are all confined, to a certain degree, by the name we have been given. But God's name cannot be said, as it is too Holy. Before this was written, as said before, his name is "I Am", and "I am that I am". Tell them that my name is "I will be with you". When Moses asked God His name God responded by telling Moses to say His name is, "I shall Be that I shall Be".* This is a literal translation of the Hebrew. This is very much akin to saying, "I am becoming". We are instructed to "...not take this Name in vain...", is like telling us to not take this idea too lightly. This could mean don't use the Name in light situations or tell lies that are given authority with the use of God's name. I believe that it also means don't just hear this Name and take it too lightly. He means, think about it. I feel, however, that it is likely to mean more than this.

The name, "I Shall Be..." has to mean "Even though I Am, I shall Be".* This has the feel of Being but also Becoming. God is infinite and perfect, so we just have to struggle with the complete meaning. He says, don't take it lightly and that we should be reverent and take it seriously. "I shall Be " has to mean that He is telling us that, even though He is, He is also becoming more Is. This is really a difficult concept to grasp for us. We probably won't fully grasp it, but I believe that, He is also telling us that He can't be contained in any box or by a defining name. We want God to be perfect, as we define perfection. God, however, is telling us that He is perfect but that He is becoming more perfect, more complete. As He defines it.

This, I feel, is very similar to the creative process that we are privileged to take part in. A truly creative artist is not necessarily preconceiving an idea but letting a living truth grow through him or her into a physical reality. It is a transformation from the spiritual/idea into the physical. This creation process may be the closest we are to understanding a part of God. After-all, our God is the Creator. In the end, we really can only contemplate Him with Faith.

I believe that, if we take the Name seriously, and contemplate what God wants for us, revelation will come into our being. If we treat Him with our greatest reverence and Holiness, then He is able to treat us as Holy. Then we will be more at one with Him.

The Fourth Commandment

> **"REMEMBER THE SABBATH DAY AND KEEP IT HOLY."**
> Exodus 20:8

The Sabbath came from God's 7th day of rest after creation. We find this recording of events in Genesis.* Even though Genesis records events before time began many scholars agree that Moses probably put the ancient remembered events in writing. Peoples in these ancient times were multiple deity worshipers and very much nature worshipers who probably responded to the cycles of the moon and sun. In other words they did not have a Sabbath per se. So where did the Sabbath

day come from? Did the moon stop? Did the sun stop?
Was any other civilization doing this at the time that
God asked this of us?

The answer to all of these questions is, No.   No
civilization had a seventh day of rest.

The Sabbath is something that God introduced to us,
His people, and has asked, and is asking, us to
participate in with Him. He rested, so He wants us to
rest. I wonder what His resting has to do with our
resting? I think that He is telling us that we are very
important to Him and that if He rests, then we too
should rest. He is not only asking the group, the tribe,
the race, the civilization to rest, but each individual. He
very often gets upset with an individual who doesn't do
as He ask so we know He is concerned with each of us.
It is a beautiful thing, if you think about it. I believe
that, the Commandments are truly the beginning of the

revelation of the uniqueness of the individual. Respecting the individual is something that had never been brought into the world before. This is the opposite of the State run civilizations in this time frame or any time frame.

It is one of the ways that God has revealed His uniqueness to us and how He has revealed how Holy we also are - made in His image. Unique.

I like to remember, or try to think of the time that the Israelites were living in when Moses led them out of Egypt. The rulers had reduced them to slavery and were not too concerned with the individual as long as they did what they were told to do. Egypt was one of the ancient civilizations that did not value the individual greatly. None of the state run civilizations did. Yet Moses led the People out of "civilization" into the wilderness, out of the status quo, out of what was accepted, out of the security of the state, to a new and unknown way and place. I think that, it was unknown to them, and probably to Moses, that God had revelation plans for them.

And so, they arrived at a place in which God decided to reveal to them where they were headed, spiritually. He first laid out the Commandments, one of which is the instruction to rest on the seventh day and to keep it Holy as "I did after creating the Heavens and the Earth".

I believe that God Himself is telling us how sacred we are by instructing us to do as He does. Rest as He does. As I write this and contemplate words I realize that the "Rest" is individual. A society or a city or a people can rest but there can't be rest until the individual rests. If, for example, each individual in a city stays in the house all day then that city is resting.

Nothing is going on. You can feel it if you go outside. It would be as quiet as a fresh snow fall. So, I believe that, the commandment to rest is to each individual and that God has, again, spoken to each one of us.

What about ..."keep it Holy"? We rest but we also need to keep it Holy. I believe that, a sacred awareness that God is here, in this day, is Holy. He makes it Holy. I think that if we are doing what He is asking us to do, that He is near. In contrast, are we keeping the day Holy when we are betting or gambling, or doing business in the Temple?

I believe that, if we contemplate God on this Holy day and do our best to listen to what He might be saying to us, individually, that would give God time to be heard. We might even hear something. I know one thing, if God were standing beside me, and He asked me to listen, and be reverent of Him, I would. If the Creator of all things asked me to listen, I would. He does ask us to keep the Sabbath holy so we should. He is trying to be close to us. He is asking us to listen.

So, I believe that, God has said that we are Holy, and that we are supposed to do as God has done and rest on the Holy day that God has created. It is definitely another relationship with Him that He expects to have with us. That He expects to have with each one of us. A Blessing!

The Fifth Commandment

> **"HONOR YOUR FATHER AND YOUR MOTHER, THAT YOU MAY LONG ENDURE ON THE LAND THAT THE LORD YOUR GOD IS GIVING YOU."**
> Exodus 20:12

This is the first commandment that has to do with how we treat each other. I believe that this again is a part of reverence for life that God seems always to be telling us to have. This commandment, to honor our parents, is a way that God is telling us to know that, we too, are worthy and honorable. We all live as a continuity of being created by our mother and father back through our ancestry all the way to God. We are at the leading edge, in our being, that has been created from Fathers and Mothers beginning with God. The spirit of God is the golden thread from creation to us. I think that God is asking us to honor this and be reverent in this creation process that we are a part of. The opposite way of looking at this is to imagine that you have no respect for yourself. In this case you surely would not honor your mother and father because they brought you into this world. If we don't honor our parents then the next step is isolation and no remembrance of what was before. Not even God. This finalizes in a dead-end. On the other hand, God seems to be telling us that if we do honor our father and mother that we will also respect ourselves, as we should, and therefore will be able to live happier and more productive lives. We will have and receive an inheritance. We will have continuity. God wants us to see that this continues the creation process. It is part of all of creation, from the beginning until the end.

We are also considering the family unit when we discuss honoring our father and our mother. Think about it. The minimum that God could be talking about in this statement is three people. Individuals. A man, a woman and a child. These three people are the basic family unit. They are, by the way in which God brings this up in the basic Ten Commandments, individuals who should honor and respect each other. He did not say "love", but "honor". I'm not sure that I know why "honor" is the word but I do know that God is telling us something by the words He uses. By respecting each other in the family unit we are able to build many family units that grow to a tribe and ultimately to a society and to a nation. And to God's people. All the way, God is telling us to love, honor and respect each other so that we "may endure long in the land that the Lord your God is giving you". To endure long says that the family unit is the very strong unit based on individual honor and respect. This unit, put together with many family units, builds the kind of civilization that God is wanting us to have. Based on the individual. Based on love.

Once again, God is showing us the love that He has for us by asking us to love each other and to be our best. He is asking us to do - what we <u>can</u> do. He is not asking us to be what we can't be. He is not <u>making</u> us do what He wants. He is asking us to be what makes us best as individuals and as a family and as a civilization. All of this, is based on love and reverence for our father, our mother, for ourselves, and for God.

God says, " that you may long endure on the land that the lord your God is giving you." I believe that, He means that if we honor our father and mother that we will have a harmonious life and will have a continuity of possession on this earth that will let us long endure with our family and in the grace of God. It also means that we will also have a family and a continued heritage that we will be blessed with.

The simplest things are such a wonderful miracle. What a wonderful thing that God wants for us.

The Sixth Commandment

"YOU SHALL NOT MURDER."
Exodus 20:13

This is the second of the commandments that has to do with how we treat each other. These last five commandments address the negative things that we may do to our neighbor. These are things that we may choose to do when we are lost and isolated. Things that we may do when we live and act selfishly and without reverence to God, or to ourselves, or to our neighbors. These are acts that we may choose to do when we deny God and exclude Him from our lives.

The many forms of murder should be considered. Right up front we should consider the fact that murder is different from killing. God has asked us to not murder but has not asked us to not kill. I really don't like to contemplate this subject because it takes me into a very negative area of life. God addresses it because it has been a problem since human life was created by Him. It does, however, signal the free choice that God has given us and is giving us.

In Genesis 4, Cain murders Abel out of jealousy. Cain wanted what Abel had, acceptance by God. He was jealous that God accepted Abel's offering. This is saying that God accepted Abel's prayers but rejected Cain's prayers. Through this story we find that God does not want us to murder and that if we do, then we will be isolated from God. We will be left as wanderers on this Earth.

There is another aspect to this recalled history that has been brought down to us. That is, why did God reject Cain's offering and prayer? The only clue we have is Gods telling Cain that "Sin couches at the door; its urge is toward you, Yet you can be its master." Apparently the offering of Cain was made while sin, probably a mind set, jealousy, was "couching at the door". I believe that, God must have meant that we can't have sinful things in our mind as we offer our prayers to Him. I believe that, God is telling us that He can't accept this. In today's everyday world we can't go out sinning on Saturday night and expect God to accept our prayers on Sunday. This story tells us that He doesn't accept our hollow prayers. And so Cain murders Abel, the innocent, in jealousy and revenge against God. This is really a story about Cain wanting things on his own terms, rather than accepting God as the creator and that the laws of God are the laws that must be followed.

So, practically speaking, if we murder then we are going to be isolated from our people and we are going to be isolated from God. I know that I'm saying these things in a very simple way. At one time it was simple. If we murdered we paid for it with our life. If we extinguished anyone else's created life by murder then we would have to be extinguished. Today we find that murder is no longer so simple. "There are circumstances", "They didn't mean to do it", "I was drunk and didn't mean to do it", "I was high on drugs and didn't know what I was doing," etc, etc. (Sin couching at the door in the mind before the act.)

In ancient times past civilizations practiced child murder and called it sacrifice to the gods. I am sure that we all agree, what an abomination that was. Today, we abort our children to pleasure and to the god of materialism. This too is an abomination and the worst kind of murder. (We are giving in to the sin couching at the door.)   I wonder how many Einstein's we have murdered?! Think about it. How many of the ancient civilizations vanished because they murdered their children? They eliminated their future to their gods, and finally, they vanished. They did not honor their fathers and their mothers.

Now modern societies are doing the same thing with their abortions. How long will it take us to vanish as we eliminate our future and, oh yes, become an abomination to God. How many does it take to become an abomination? One? Two? Millions?

God tells us to not murder. We have no understanding of this unless we walk back from this statement to understanding what leads us to this, and what God is really saying. God is not asking us to discount our physical lives. He is telling us to know that the spiritual life and our relation to Him is part of our total being.

God has said, "Hear oh Israel, the Lord Thy God is One.* We are made in His image, He wants us to accept that. He wants us to be at one with ourselves, like He is at one with Himself.

Murder is the result, a final act, of denying that God, Is. The final act of living a life away from God. A final act of living an irreverent life. A final act of living a materialistic selfish life. A final act of denying the value of the individual, an individual.

The Seventh Commandment

"YOU SHALL NOT COMMIT ADULTERY."
Exodus 20:13

I believe that, adultery is an all inclusive word. Even if we look up the Hebrew word for adultery we don't find any hints as to the meaning of this statement outside of the direct words. One thing is obvious. God does not want a married man to have a sexual relationship with another woman. The Hebrew word used in this commandment, Na'aph*, has its meaning to be concerning a married man and a married woman. Well, why would God have such a law or a rule for us to live by? I think that, we must consider the results of the action as to what God must mean. I believe that results are the key to understanding this commandment.

The result of adultery leads away from God. It leads us away from the ways that God wants us to live our lives. First of all trust, the unique love bond, the singular commitment that your spouse is the most important person in the world is both a secular commitment and a blessing from God. The breaking of the marriage promise, to take care of each other, no matter what, is breaking a commitment with your spouse and God. The lie of adultery, and the breaking of the promise that was made before God, (this is denying God's will) in effect breaks the family unit that is the basis for family and race. The effect of this is the breaking of the Fifth Commandment to "Honor your Father and your Mother".

In addition, adultery is also the using of another person as only an object on a pure animal instinct basis, to throw away for something "better", if and when it comes along. And it will come along. This, I believe, is reducing this other person to something less than one of God's created people, something less than Holy. By doing this we are denying God's created, and denying God, by making what God created less than what he or she is.

Then we have the possible child, an offspring. Who's child is it? What happens to the child? Let's say that a child is born from this relationship. As we follow this spiral down we will immediately run into the question of abortion. Another word for murder. Then there is the question of how to get rid of the spouse. Some have chosen murder at this junction. So, we are following a spiral even further into the pit as we are selling our soul. Then what? This is one branch of the spider web that is being brought into being that we are likely not to survive. Oh, we might live, but we may not survive.

I believe that we also have to consider what is happening to us spiritually, if we go down this path. In this situation we are losing the spiritual relationship that is between God and each individual and between God and each married couple.

Spirituality is involved with love. True love is a gift from God. A part of God. Our ability to love is one of the things that is a part of God. One of the clues to God. So, when we sell our soul, this is saying that we are selling our ability to love. We are selling the love that is of God. These are really such obvious things that so many of us are so easily, ready to throw away. Remember, God wants us to be the person that He created. To be our most Holy in His light. Adultery throws this away.

In adultery, we are being untruthful to our spouse. We are having to live a lie in order to have "love" outside of our marriage. So, *the lie* leads to treating our spouse, and eventually the other woman, irreverently. I also think that living a lie is a way of treating oneself irreverently. So, we would be treating three of God's creations as though they were less than Holy. The man is treating the women as a thing, and himself, less than human. He is treating his spouse without respect. Then if there is a child, as mentioned above, then we will treat the child as less than one of God's Holy people. So now we have involved four of God's created people as something less than Holy. This is another denial of God. In fact, this is what the evil one is wanting us to do as we sell our soul.

God is always wanting us to be better than this and to live to the highest ideals. Not abstractly, but applied to specific situations. He knows better than us, that all things, all deeds, lead somewhere. There is really no isolation in living. All things are connected. All things are one.

We are supposed to be more than this, as God's created. And so, God has asked us not to commit adultery.

The Eighth Commandment

"YOU SHALL NOT STEAL."
Exodus 20:13

This statement from God, to us, is asking us not to steal. This is not too complicated, on the face of it. By asking us, God is telling us that this is one of the actions that leads to all kinds of things that take us away from Him, and away from our fellow man, and away from ourselves. I believe that, God is telling us that this leads us down a path that is hard to come back from. This, stealing, is a door that *evil* comes in through. This is a door, through which *evil* presents to us, that we have to make a choice about.

God is telling us to make the choice. God would not even have to ask us to not steal if there were not always the temptation to the easy way. *Evil* always offers us an easy way to sell our soul. I think that this is one of the ways that the *lie* expresses itself. There is always the possibility to steal so there is always a time to choose. When we choose not to steal, we are choosing God. We are choosing God because we are choosing a way of life that keeps us close to God and keeps our soul and spirit in tact. On the other hand, if we choose to steal, we are then choosing to go away from God.

In secular areas, getting caught, is the reference point. "If we are not caught, then we didn't steal." But this is not true because we are living in a relationship with

God. The act itself is what causes us to separate from our Creator. But does it matter? Yes. We lose a little bit of soul when we do this. When we lose soul then other things become easier to do and we progress into the pit. We live the lie.

Specifically, there are many forms of stealing. Overtly we can just take something that belongs to someone else. But we can also steal ideas, inventions, private knowledge, intellectual property, cheat on a test, steal an education record, steal an election, etc., etc., etc. The list is endless. Sooner or later the shell we are building is not even us. We can borrow $5 and never pay it back. Next we can borrow $100 and never pay that back. Then we just have a tendency to take what we want rather than earn it. Then, we begin to not trust anyone and then, not even ourselves. Why would we trust ourselves? We know that we steal. And if we steal, then "I bet everyone is stealing." So, then, we can't trust anyone. Each step is further into the pit. A vortex that becomes harder and harder to escape. Then, the evil one has a good hold on us. Choices become more in relation to the *evil one* than to our Creator.

We lose respect for ourselves each time we steal or do something that we know God does not want us to do. The loss of self respect seems to transfer out of us into an attitude of disrespect for others. At some point, we can't even believe in God because of this, simply as a self defense mechanism. This also tends to lead to isolation and away from the social context that we live in. It really only gets worse.

Let's imagine a small example of stealing. A child takes a sandwich out of a classmates backpack because his Mom forgot to pack one for him. "Well that was easy, if I want to I can just do that for lunch. Kind of exciting, anyway. We are still friends because he doesn't know I took it." Next thing you know, the child is a little older, he sees a skateboard he likes that a neighbor kid is riding. "Mom said that she wouldn't get me one, so I will just borrow this for awhile", he thinks. "I will sell this so that I can buy one of my own." So he sells what he stole so that he "honestly" can buy one for himself. So, here we go, next it is a car, and then taking money from an individual. Oh yes, the person who he asked to give him his wallet hesitates, so, he just kills him. Now we have murder, and the *evil one* is really happy, as we descend even further into the pit. Or maybe the stakes just get "higher" and he decides to rob a bank. While he is there he might just have to murder three people. After all, someone might have seen him. Right?

Then we have this same kid who learned, way back when, that he could talk other kids into wanting him to give him things in exchange for a promise. Here are the people selling us worthless stock certificates and promising big returns in the future. There seems to be an endless stream of white collar ideas of how to steal.

Let's go back to concepts for a minute here. Stealing is really about power. The will of an individual over another individual or the will of rulers over people and the will of nations over nations. The fight for domination. There are so many historical examples. If we could just learn. Every example, has led away from God. Every example of a nation stealing from other nations and peoples has ultimately led to the failure of the powerful and the stealing nations. Rome is a good example of the most powerful nation in existence during its time. It survived for so long relying on power and might. Any perceived threat, it eliminated. It kept all of its gods and ended up Godless. It finally ended up being eliminated from the face of the earth. And the

Romans were taken down by barbarians who decided that they were not going to be dominated.

I believe this is the whole point from God to us. He wants us to be our best, reverent and Holy, and He knows that an act, such as stealing, keeps us from this. Obviously, He is not going to make us do anything. He is more or less advising us, as to what we do, as to its rewards or consequences. I believe that God must be in an awful lot of sorrow because of some of the choices that we make. He is the God of Love and seems to never quit trying to get us, or keep us, in the right path to our own happiness and Holiness.

So, I believe that, stealing is a big deal. The stealing mind set leads us totally away from our loving God and into the false promises of materialism for its own sake and then into the whole power struggle, from us to nations.

God never gives up on us. He is always hoping that we will wake up and realize that we need to turn around. To make the full turning. When we do, He is always waiting on us.

So, God has a lot to say when He says, "Don't steal".

The Ninth Commandment

> **"THOU SHALL NOT BEAR FALSE WITNESS."**
> Exodus 20:14

This is a commandment about lying. About living the Lie. If we think about it, there are at least three people and God referred to this statement. There has to be someone listening that one is witnessing to. There has to be the one who is witnessing. There has to be the one that is witnessed about. God is there among them all. This commandment involves other people. So this is a societal thing as well as an individual thing. This statement states the desire of God, in this situation, that we should be honest in all of our doings and relations.

So, we should not lie, but also, we should not lie about anyone that in such a way it will do them harm or help them at the detriment to someone else. To bear witness also involves God because being a witness often implies that we are telling the truth, "under God." Without God involved there is no Truth. All other is relative and related to consequences. Truth related to God is a more absolute ideal related to acceptance by God. All of the commandments are this. If we break any of the commandments we are lying about something. We are being dishonest about something. We might be breaking a contract by something that we are doing which means that we are being dishonest about some promise that we made.

You know, this addressing an action, and way of being, by Man was set down to Noah after the Flood. All civilizations have Flood stories. There is a lot of speculation about this but we do know, it was a long time ago. The point that I'm trying to make is that mankind has been fighting the lying problem for a long time. After thousands of years, we have, at least learned, that there are many forms of lying and that none of them are for the betterment of Man. God said it in such simple terms. I believe that, by stating this so simply, it becomes universal. We think up so many different ways to do almost anything. Along with that we think up many ways to lie. So, we make it complex, in our own minds, and by our own actions. And by our own choices.

I want to keep this as plain as possible so I thought that it would be good to think about what the Lie can be. It can be deception, disguise, forgery, lie by omission, less than the whole truth, misrepresentation, propaganda, perjury, misleading, and exaggeration or puffery. "But so what. It's the bottom line that counts at any cost. Right?"

When it comes to God, and progressing spiritually, wrong!

So, what about daily living? For example if we witness for anyone, friend or foe, we should not give a false statement. To be a witness is not just to be a witness in court but to witness in our every day lives. We can't act and talk as a knowledgeable person about something in our daily lives when we don't know anything about the subject that we are talking, witnessing, about, if we are to live as God wants us to live. I know, it is hard to sell anything without a little honey added to whatever we are selling; but do we have to? Deception is a way we get involved, from time to time. Corporations have learned how to make us think that there are so many reasons to buy their stock, for example, by way of ads, by way of outside source blogs or newsletters or whatever, when the true value is different than what they have made us think. They have sold us by deception even though they have followed all of the securities laws. An individual can deceive another individual by selling stock in a company on the promise that it is going to gain certain contracts, that in reality, it doesn't have a chance to achieve. So he has deceived with false promises.

The key to this Commandment statement is "false witness". This is another way of saying, "Do not lie". All lies involve our neighbor. This is another choice that we have to make in our lives. A choice to be with God and live the way that He asks us to live. God knows that when we lie we are also lying against ourselves. We lose honor, we are not honest and we are not truthful. These all lead us away from our individual self respect and confidence. We become less of a person, the person, than what God wants us to be. We become less responsible for all of our actions and thoughts. God is leading us to and giving us the will to be responsible in

His desire for us to be the best that we can be. One of the elements that we have to maintain is, "Do not Lie".

I think that this desire of God, that we should not lie, even in order to protect a friend or to harm an enemy is to keep us from straying away from Him. If we lie, we are moving away from how God wants us to be, and moving away from Him in the process.

I believe that He wants us to be near to Him and that He is telling us the ways that we can do this. Included with this is how we treat our neighbor. He is asking us to treat our neighbor with respect and as one of His created. We can't treat a neighbor in a bad way and turn around and pretend that we are treating God with reverence. It all goes together.

Once again, "The Lord Thy God Is One."

The Tenth Commandment

> **"YOU SHALL NOT COVET YOUR NEIGHBOR'S HOUSE: YOU SHALL NOT COVET YOUR NEIGHBOR'S WIFE, OR HIS MALE OR FEMALE SLAVE, OR HIS OX OR HIS ASS, OR ANYTHING THAT IS YOUR NEIGHBOR'S."**
> Exodus 20:14

This desire of God for us, revealed in this statement given to Moses 3,400 years ago,* plus or minus, is about our heart and soul. It is about the conflict between good and evil and about the choices that we have to make. It is also about the fact that God has given, and is giving, us a choice in this life. The prime choices are about choosing Him or choosing the evil way. At all times God is speaking to us, as individuals,

individuals!, and the direction that He knows is best for us. He definitely wants our individual free choice, not a choice out of fear. He has given, and gives, us the choice, out of Love for us. He wants us to freely choose, out of love for Him.

I think that, God wants us to be aware of our relations with everyone we are living with in this life. I always have to remember that God is so far ahead of us and that He has said something that has meaning down to the core of a certain aspect of our life and to every aspect of our life. Just because we read or hear a statement from God doesn't mean that we understand the intent. The words always stand mutely there. Challenging us to understand. To contemplate.

In ancient times, the prophet says things that he doesn't necessarily understand but that he relays because God has asked him to relay it. Then those words stand for us to think about, and contemplate. Moses was the prophet. Even so, the words remain, at all times, universal and contemporary.

In many ways this statement, not to covet, is much like saying, "Know thyself". I believe that, God is telling us, on one level, that we should know what we have, and know what we want. I think that He is saying, don't want what someone else has, just because he has it, but know what we want and be happy with what we have. Be happy with what we have been given. In relation to this, I believe that God wants us to set our own goals and do that. We are all guilty of wanting what our neighbors have. Our natural instinct is to have as much as "they" have. It doesn't matter if we need it or not. I believe that this is not what God wants because he knows the sources from where this is coming from, and where it is going.

I believe, though, that God is really talking about our motives. Where do the motives come from? Where or what are the motives going to lead to? Sure, we shouldn't want what our neighbor has, but the desire, the coveting, that gives rise to these things goes to the heart of us. Desire, lust, and to covet, are not things in themselves, but are a state of mind, the basis of intent. ("Sin couching at the door.")

Remember, God is asking us to think, and do, from His way. I believe that, this state of mind, to covet, is not from God but from Evil. So, when God asks us not to covet He is asking us not to think in a way that comes from the forces that are not from Him. Coveting, in other words, is a state of mind that is against God.

Where does coveting lead? Like everything else in life, everything starts in small steps, leading down, or up, paths to destinations we may or may not want.

Coveting is, lust, greed, envy, and desire. These state of mind realities lead to falsehood and *the lie.* Specifically, then, coveting can lead to murder, adultery, stealing and lying. Next, it leads to hate, to prejudice, and to dishonor, driven by the minds ability to covet. From Cain to us.

On the other hand, making the choice, to not covet, frees us to be honorable, to be giving, to be loving, to be forgiving, to be thankful, to be happy. To be in tune with God. To be with God.

In today's world, where so many things are so easy, let us consider some paths to disaster as a result of coveting. If, for example, an individual is making an income per month that allows only so much for the necessities for living. (I know that we all know this, but, let's follow this thread.) The individual sees that some of his/her, (he), friends are buying this, buying that, and he wants to live that way too. Then comes a credit card. Not a bad thing in itself, but a thing that can lead to many negative consequences. He sees this as a way to keep up with his friends. So he buys a few things on credit. Before he knows it he is only able to make interest payments without paying the debt down. Then interest rates change, all the stuff that he has purchased is starting to wear out, the economy goes into recession, he loses his job and has to take a pay cut at a new job. Now what? Things are getting tighter. Then, he can't keep up with the payments on his credit card and other things. You know, in our world, this is a scene repeated over and over and over. In the ancient world people became slaves to repay debt. I think that, we too become slaves to the things that we want, or think that we want, just to keep up. This is getting worse though, people are really losing their houses, losing their cars, and losing hope for any kind of good future. And living under bridges. Does this come from God? I think not. This comes from the other side. The Evil that thrives on suffering.

So here the "credit man" is. There is never a time for, no choice. If you think about it, if we make no choice we have made the choice to make no choice. Something that *evil* wants. Like I said, here is the person at a place for new decisions, new choices.

Another example. Let's take one scene that we have all read about in the newspaper or have seen on TV. "The individual lost his spouse to a random shooting." Later we find that it wasn't random at all. "Police have found a link between the gunman and the husband. There was insurance, he was in great debt. He denies it." Then, "There is a suicide." So evil has triumphed again using the tool of coveting as the vehicle.

What about the "big boys"? They are really no different. We have all read about the men on the top who, because of their wealth, believe that they can do anything that they please. There was a man, very "smart", who ponzied his way to billions of dollars. In the end he was caught because of the same recession as the "credit man" above and could not make payments to the investors. He is now in prison. He was a slave to his own greed. I am sure that any of us can think of enumerable cases similar to these two that have led to either murder, stealing, adultery, etc as a result of coveting. Selfishness. Possessed by evil.*

I believe that God is simply asking us to think, and do, in such a way that keeps us free from going down these paths. If we don't covet then we are not tempted. I know, we are human, temptation is always presenting itself and we always have choices to make.

I believe that He is always with us when we need the strength to make the correct decision. I also believe that He is the spiritual awakening of Love in us if we choose His ways. He is not asking us to live a life of denial but asking us to live a life of positive creativity and fulfillment. This is the way to happiness and fulfillment, that God is offering, if we just seek and make this choice to living. A state of Giving.

I think that I would rather concentrate on the positive aspects of this Tenth Commandment statement instead of negatives. If we don't covet or lust, then what happens? I think that, a lot of people, that we never read about in the newspaper, or see on TV, are living this good life. I would bet that you know people who are living a comfortable life. People who seem to be in tune with their life. They are happy with God, their spouse, their children and their family. They are productive and contribute to their world. They are very secure with their understanding of God in their revelation walk.

I feel that, this all must have to do with the renewal of life. In many ways, every moment is a renewal - a becoming. We have new revelations every day. Everyday we are like newborns as we gain knowledge. Moses asked God His name and received the revelation that, "I Am that I Am". "I shall be that I shall Be." "I Am Becoming...". * So, I believe that, God is telling us to be like Him, by asking us to follow His ways, and know that we must be ever new born and becoming something new as we add to and receive what we can be. Revelation comes in quiet small steps, I think. We must at times be silent and listen. The Shema, "Hear Oh Israel, The Lord Thy God Is One." is one of the greatest revelations of all time. More in today's time, Hear Oh People, The Lord Thy God, Is One.

What a wondrous thing, that God, the Creator of all things, including us, is asking us to live, and be, in a certain way that He knows we can be. Why else would He ask us if He did not know that we could be as He is asking us to be? The fact that He asks us tells us that we can do it. When I think about the fact that, He Created us in His Image, that this is what He is trying to get us to realize and be.

"I believe oh Lord, please help my unbelief". *

And so, He is here for us, and He is asking us to be here for Him.

Conclusion

The Ten Commandments, statements from God to us, His people, has given us revelation about God and about ourselves. God has told us that He has chosen us as His people. He has told us that He wants us to accept Him. He has told us the things that we need to do to be accepted by Him.

He has told us that we are special and that we are Holy as He is Holy. (In His image.) He has asked us to be responsible for our Holiness. In this regard He has instructed us on how to treat our neighbor. He has also instructed us on how we should be reverent to Him.

God has given us, with the Commandments, a way to achieve happiness and fulfillment on this earth as we live and breath with Him at our side.

I believe that He is also instructing us on our revelation journey and helping us on our development into Becoming, as He is Becoming.

He has told us that we have been created in His image. Because of that, we are also Becoming in His image just as He is Becoming.

Reference Notes

Page 5
"scholars and intellectuals and clergy", Philo Judaeus of Alexandria, A Treatise Concerning the Ten Commandments
RamBam, Maimonides, The Guide of the Perplexed
Martin Luther, "Table Talk"

Page 7
hard wired evolutionary, "Origin of the Species", Darwin

Page 9
"The Ten Commandments", Torah, JPS, 1967

Page 14
what His name is, Exodus 3:14

Page 17
He has told us that very directly. 1st Commandment

Page 34 & 35 3rd Commandment
"I shall Be that I shall Be". Exodus 3:14

"Even though I Am, I shall Be". Hebrew word, Eleyeh-Asher-Elheyeh

Page 37
events in Genesis. Genesis 2:3

Page 51
"couching at the door". Genesis 4:7 "A Treatise Concerning The Ten Commandments",   Philo

Page 54
"Hear oh Israel, the Lord Thy God is One. " Deuteronomy 6:4-9 Torah, The Holy Bible, Cambridge University Press, Mark 6

Page 55
"Na'aph" Hebrew, adultery, Hebrew Dictionary

Page 75
Moses 3,400 years ago,* Wikipedia Dictionary, Moses, history

Page 84
"Hear oh Israel, the Lord Thy God is One.*, Deuteronomy 6:4-9 Torah

Page 85
"I believe oh Lord, please help my unbelief". *   Mark 9:24
The Holy Bible, Cambridge University Press

Reference Concepts

Love:
   The Love of God is an all encompassing spiritual Love.
Discovery Mission:
   Refers to the enlightenment of the spirit and soul.
Enlightened:
   Realization in mind and spirit of the presence of God.
Becoming:
   The path to enlightenment and Revelation of God.
I Am:
   God's self declared existence.
Man:
   All of Mankind.
Revelation
   Awareness of the truth of God.
Holy:
   That which is of God or has been touched by God.
Evil:
   That which is against God and seeks to destroy God's people.
The Lie:
   All untruths that seeks to live in deception and evil.
Graven:
   Man made things that people worship.
Covet:
   To lust after anything without right.
Idol:
   Person or thing that people put above God.
Superstition:
   Beliefs that people hold that have nothing to do with God.
Possessed:
   Overcome with spirits or beliefs that are not of God.